50 Recipes from the Farm for Home

By: Kelly Johnson

Table of Contents

- Farmhouse Vegetable Soup
- Classic Beef Stew with Root Vegetables
- Hearty Chicken and Dumplings
- Farm-Fresh Salad with Mixed Greens and Herbs
- Rustic Potato Leek Soup
- Homemade Cornbread with Honey Butter
- Roasted Chicken with Garlic and Herbs
- Creamy Mashed Potatoes
- Fresh Garden Ratatouille
- Grilled Pork Chops with Apple Chutney
- Slow Cooker Beef Pot Roast
- Savory Sausage and Pepper Skillet
- Buttermilk Biscuits with Sausage Gravy
- Farmhouse Macaroni and Cheese
- Baked Beans with Bacon
- Lemon Herb Roasted Chicken
- Corn Chowder with Bacon
- Zucchini and Tomato Frittata
- Honey Glazed Carrots
- Beef and Vegetable Stir-Fry
- Apple Crisp with Oats and Cinnamon
- Farmhouse Meatloaf with Tomato Glaze
- Cucumber and Tomato Salad with Balsamic Vinaigrette
- Creamy Chicken and Mushroom Pasta
- Roasted Root Vegetables with Thyme
- Farm-Fresh Strawberry Shortcake
- Slow Cooker Pulled Pork Sandwiches
- Garlic Herb Roasted Potatoes
- Grilled Vegetable Platter with Herb Butter
- Classic Farmhouse Pancakes with Maple Syrup
- Chicken and Rice Casserole
- Fresh Berry Cobbler
- Skillet Cornbread with Jalapenos and Cheddar
- Spinach and Cheese Stuffed Chicken Breast
- Farmhouse Chili with Beans and Cornbread Muffins

- Grilled Corn on the Cob with Chili Lime Butter
- Creamy Mushroom Risotto
- Apple Cinnamon Oatmeal
- Farmhouse Quiche with Ham and Cheese
- Maple Glazed Bacon
- Fresh Garden Salad with Homemade Dressing
- Baked Ham with Brown Sugar Glaze
- Butternut Squash Soup with Crispy Sage
- Garlic Butter Shrimp Pasta
- Farmhouse Beef and Vegetable Stew
- Roasted Brussels Sprouts with Bacon and Balsamic Glaze
- Grilled Chicken Caesar Salad
- Farm-Fresh Blueberry Muffins
- Sweet and Spicy Barbecue Ribs
- Pumpkin Pie with Whipped Cream

Farmhouse Vegetable Soup

Ingredients:

- 2 tablespoons olive oil
- 1 onion, diced
- 2 carrots, peeled and diced
- 2 celery stalks, diced
- 2 cloves garlic, minced
- 2 potatoes, peeled and diced
- 1 zucchini, diced
- 1 cup green beans, trimmed and chopped
- 1 can (400g) diced tomatoes
- 4 cups vegetable broth or chicken broth
- 1 teaspoon dried thyme
- 1 teaspoon dried oregano
- Salt and pepper, to taste
- Fresh parsley, chopped, for garnish (optional)

Instructions:

1. Heat the olive oil in a large pot or Dutch oven over medium heat.
2. Add the diced onion, carrots, and celery to the pot. Cook, stirring occasionally, until the vegetables are softened, about 5 minutes.
3. Add the minced garlic to the pot and cook for an additional minute, until fragrant.
4. Stir in the diced potatoes, zucchini, green beans, diced tomatoes, vegetable broth, dried thyme, and dried oregano.
5. Season the soup with salt and pepper to taste.
6. Bring the soup to a boil, then reduce the heat to low. Cover the pot and let the soup simmer for about 20-25 minutes, or until the vegetables are tender.
7. Taste the soup and adjust the seasoning if needed.
8. Ladle the farmhouse vegetable soup into bowls and garnish with chopped fresh parsley, if desired.
9. Serve the soup hot, accompanied by crusty bread or crackers.

Enjoy your homemade farmhouse vegetable soup as a delicious and wholesome meal, perfect for any time of the year!

Classic Beef Stew with Root Vegetables

Ingredients:

- 1.5 kg stewing beef, cut into bite-sized pieces
- 2 tablespoons olive oil
- 2 onions, chopped
- 4 cloves garlic, minced
- 4 carrots, peeled and cut into chunks
- 4 parsnips, peeled and cut into chunks
- 4 celery stalks, chopped
- 2 potatoes, peeled and cut into chunks
- 2 tablespoons tomato paste
- 4 cups beef broth
- 2 cups red wine (optional)
- 2 bay leaves
- 1 teaspoon dried thyme
- 1 teaspoon dried rosemary
- Salt and pepper, to taste
- Chopped fresh parsley, for garnish (optional)

Instructions:

1. In a large pot or Dutch oven, heat the olive oil over medium-high heat.
2. Season the beef pieces with salt and pepper. Working in batches, brown the beef on all sides in the hot oil. Remove the browned beef from the pot and set aside.
3. Add the chopped onions to the pot and cook until softened, about 5 minutes. Add the minced garlic and cook for an additional minute.
4. Return the browned beef to the pot. Add the chopped carrots, parsnips, celery, and potatoes.
5. Stir in the tomato paste, beef broth, red wine (if using), bay leaves, dried thyme, and dried rosemary.
6. Bring the stew to a boil, then reduce the heat to low. Cover the pot and let the stew simmer for about 2 hours, stirring occasionally, or until the beef is tender.
7. Taste the stew and adjust the seasoning with salt and pepper, if needed.
8. Once the beef and vegetables are cooked through and tender, remove the bay leaves from the stew.

9. Ladle the classic beef stew with root vegetables into bowls and garnish with chopped fresh parsley, if desired.
10. Serve the stew hot, accompanied by crusty bread or mashed potatoes.

Enjoy your homemade classic beef stew with root vegetables as a comforting and satisfying meal, perfect for sharing with family and friends!

Hearty Chicken and Dumplings

Ingredients:

For the Chicken Stew:

- 1 kg chicken thighs, bone-in and skin-on
- Salt and pepper, to taste
- 2 tablespoons olive oil
- 2 onions, chopped
- 4 carrots, peeled and sliced
- 4 celery stalks, sliced
- 4 cloves garlic, minced
- 1/4 cup all-purpose flour
- 6 cups chicken broth
- 2 bay leaves
- 1 teaspoon dried thyme
- 1 teaspoon dried rosemary
- 1 cup frozen peas
- Chopped fresh parsley, for garnish (optional)

For the Dumplings:

- 2 cups all-purpose flour
- 1 tablespoon baking powder
- 1 teaspoon salt
- 1/4 cup cold unsalted butter, cut into small cubes
- 3/4 cup milk

Instructions:

1. Season the chicken thighs generously with salt and pepper.
2. In a large Dutch oven or pot, heat the olive oil over medium-high heat. Add the chicken thighs, skin side down, and cook until golden brown, about 5 minutes per side. Remove the chicken from the pot and set aside.

3. In the same pot, add the chopped onions, carrots, celery, and minced garlic. Cook, stirring occasionally, until the vegetables are softened, about 5 minutes.
4. Sprinkle the flour over the vegetables in the pot and stir to coat. Cook for 1-2 minutes to cook out the raw taste of the flour.
5. Slowly pour in the chicken broth while stirring constantly to prevent lumps from forming. Add the bay leaves, dried thyme, and dried rosemary.
6. Return the browned chicken thighs to the pot, along with any juices that have accumulated. Bring the stew to a simmer, then reduce the heat to low. Cover the pot and let the stew simmer gently for about 45 minutes, or until the chicken is cooked through and tender.
7. While the stew is simmering, prepare the dumplings. In a large mixing bowl, whisk together the flour, baking powder, and salt. Cut in the cold butter using a pastry cutter or fork until the mixture resembles coarse crumbs. Gradually add the milk, stirring until a soft dough forms.
8. Once the chicken is cooked through and tender, remove it from the pot and shred the meat using two forks. Discard the bones and skin.
9. Return the shredded chicken to the pot, along with the frozen peas. Stir to combine.
10. Drop spoonfuls of the dumpling dough onto the surface of the simmering stew, spacing them evenly apart. Cover the pot and let the dumplings cook for about 15 minutes, or until they are cooked through and fluffy.
11. Once the dumplings are cooked, remove the pot from the heat. Sprinkle the chopped fresh parsley over the top of the stew, if desired.
12. Serve the hearty chicken and dumplings hot, ladled into bowls.

Enjoy your homemade hearty chicken and dumplings as a comforting and satisfying meal!

Farm-Fresh Salad with Mixed Greens and Herbs

Ingredients:

For the Salad:

- 6 cups mixed salad greens (such as lettuce, spinach, arugula, and kale), washed and torn into bite-sized pieces
- 1 cup fresh herbs (such as parsley, basil, cilantro, and dill), chopped
- 1 cup cherry tomatoes, halved
- 1 cucumber, sliced
- 1 bell pepper, thinly sliced
- 1/2 red onion, thinly sliced
- 1/4 cup crumbled feta cheese (optional)
- 1/4 cup toasted nuts or seeds (such as almonds, walnuts, or sunflower seeds) (optional)

For the Dressing:

- 1/4 cup extra virgin olive oil
- 2 tablespoons balsamic vinegar
- 1 tablespoon Dijon mustard
- 1 teaspoon honey
- Salt and pepper, to taste

Instructions:

1. In a large salad bowl, combine the mixed salad greens and chopped fresh herbs.
2. Add the halved cherry tomatoes, sliced cucumber, thinly sliced bell pepper, and thinly sliced red onion to the salad bowl.
3. If using, sprinkle the crumbled feta cheese and toasted nuts or seeds over the top of the salad.
4. In a small jar or bowl, combine the extra virgin olive oil, balsamic vinegar, Dijon mustard, honey, salt, and pepper. Shake or whisk until well combined.
5. Drizzle the dressing over the salad, tossing gently to coat all the ingredients.

6. Taste the salad and adjust the seasoning with salt and pepper, if needed.
7. Serve the farm-fresh salad with mixed greens and herbs immediately, garnished with additional fresh herbs if desired.

Enjoy your homemade farm-fresh salad as a delicious and nutritious side dish or light meal!

Rustic Potato Leek Soup

Ingredients:

- 3 large leeks, white and light green parts only, washed and thinly sliced
- 3 tablespoons unsalted butter
- 3 cloves garlic, minced
- 4 large potatoes, peeled and diced
- 6 cups vegetable broth or chicken broth
- 1 bay leaf
- 1 teaspoon dried thyme
- Salt and pepper, to taste
- 1/2 cup heavy cream (optional)
- Chopped fresh chives, for garnish (optional)

Instructions:

1. In a large pot or Dutch oven, melt the butter over medium heat. Add the sliced leeks and minced garlic to the pot. Cook, stirring occasionally, until the leeks are softened, about 5-7 minutes.
2. Add the diced potatoes to the pot, along with the vegetable broth or chicken broth, bay leaf, and dried thyme. Season with salt and pepper to taste.
3. Bring the soup to a boil, then reduce the heat to low. Cover the pot and let the soup simmer gently for about 20-25 minutes, or until the potatoes are tender.
4. Once the potatoes are cooked through, remove the bay leaf from the soup.
5. Using an immersion blender, puree the soup until smooth and creamy. Alternatively, you can transfer the soup in batches to a blender and blend until smooth, then return it to the pot.
6. If using, stir in the heavy cream to add richness to the soup. Taste and adjust the seasoning with salt and pepper, if needed.
7. Serve the rustic potato leek soup hot, garnished with chopped fresh chives if desired.

Enjoy your homemade rustic potato leek soup as a comforting and satisfying meal!

Homemade Cornbread with Honey Butter

Ingredients:

For the Cornbread:

- 1 cup cornmeal
- 1 cup all-purpose flour
- 1/4 cup granulated sugar
- 1 tablespoon baking powder
- 1 teaspoon salt
- 1 cup buttermilk
- 2 large eggs
- 1/4 cup unsalted butter, melted

For the Honey Butter:

- 1/2 cup unsalted butter, softened
- 2 tablespoons honey
- Pinch of salt (optional)

Instructions:

1. Preheat your oven to 200°C (400°F). Grease a 9-inch square baking dish or a cast iron skillet.
2. In a large mixing bowl, whisk together the cornmeal, all-purpose flour, sugar, baking powder, and salt until well combined.
3. In a separate bowl, whisk together the buttermilk, eggs, and melted butter until smooth.
4. Pour the wet ingredients into the dry ingredients and stir until just combined. Be careful not to overmix.
5. Pour the batter into the prepared baking dish or skillet, spreading it out evenly.
6. Bake the cornbread in the preheated oven for 20-25 minutes, or until golden brown and a toothpick inserted into the center comes out clean.

7. While the cornbread is baking, prepare the honey butter. In a small bowl, mix together the softened butter and honey until smooth. Add a pinch of salt if desired.
8. Once the cornbread is baked, remove it from the oven and let it cool for a few minutes before slicing.
9. Serve the warm cornbread slices with a dollop of honey butter on top.

Enjoy your homemade cornbread with honey butter as a delicious and comforting treat!

Roasted Chicken with Garlic and Herbs

Ingredients:

- 1 whole chicken (about 1.5 to 2 kg), giblets removed
- 4 cloves garlic, minced
- 2 tablespoons fresh herbs (such as rosemary, thyme, and parsley), chopped
- 2 tablespoons olive oil
- 1 lemon, halved
- Salt and pepper, to taste

Instructions:

1. Preheat your oven to 200°C (400°F).
2. Rinse the chicken under cold water and pat it dry with paper towels.
3. In a small bowl, mix together the minced garlic, chopped fresh herbs, olive oil, salt, and pepper to form a paste.
4. Carefully loosen the skin of the chicken by gently sliding your fingers between the skin and the meat, being careful not to tear the skin.
5. Rub the garlic and herb paste all over the chicken, both under the skin and on the outside, making sure to coat it evenly.
6. Place the lemon halves inside the cavity of the chicken.
7. Tie the legs of the chicken together with kitchen twine and tuck the wings underneath the body.
8. Place the chicken breast-side up on a roasting rack set inside a roasting pan.
9. Roast the chicken in the preheated oven for 1 to 1.5 hours, or until the juices run clear when the thickest part of the thigh is pierced with a skewer or a meat thermometer inserted into the thickest part of the thigh registers 75°C (165°F).
10. Once the chicken is cooked through and golden brown, remove it from the oven and let it rest for 10-15 minutes before carving.
11. Carve the roasted chicken into serving pieces and serve hot, accompanied by your favorite sides such as roasted vegetables, mashed potatoes, or a fresh salad.

Enjoy your homemade roasted chicken with garlic and herbs as a delicious and comforting meal!

Creamy Mashed Potatoes

Ingredients:

- 2 kg potatoes (such as Russet or Yukon Gold), peeled and cut into chunks
- Salt, for boiling water
- 1/2 cup unsalted butter, cut into cubes
- 1 cup whole milk or heavy cream, warmed
- Salt and pepper, to taste
- Chopped fresh chives or parsley, for garnish (optional)

Instructions:

1. Place the potato chunks in a large pot and cover them with cold water. Add a generous pinch of salt to the water.
2. Bring the water to a boil over high heat, then reduce the heat to medium-low and simmer the potatoes for 15-20 minutes, or until they are fork-tender.
3. Drain the cooked potatoes in a colander and return them to the pot.
4. Add the cubed butter to the pot with the hot potatoes. Let the butter melt slightly.
5. Mash the potatoes and butter together using a potato masher or a fork until the butter is evenly distributed and the potatoes are mashed to your desired consistency.
6. Gradually add the warm milk or cream to the mashed potatoes, stirring continuously, until the desired creaminess is achieved. You may not need to use all of the milk or cream, so add it gradually and stop when you reach your desired consistency.
7. Season the mashed potatoes with salt and pepper to taste. Be sure to taste and adjust the seasoning as needed.
8. Transfer the creamy mashed potatoes to a serving bowl.
9. If desired, garnish the mashed potatoes with chopped fresh chives or parsley for a pop of color and flavor.
10. Serve the creamy mashed potatoes hot, alongside your favorite main dishes.

Enjoy your homemade creamy mashed potatoes as a delicious and comforting side dish!

Fresh Garden Ratatouille

Ingredients:

- 2 tablespoons olive oil
- 1 onion, diced
- 3 cloves garlic, minced
- 1 eggplant, diced
- 2 zucchini, diced
- 2 bell peppers, diced (use a mix of colors for visual appeal)
- 2 tomatoes, diced
- 1 can (400g) crushed tomatoes
- 1 teaspoon dried thyme
- 1 teaspoon dried oregano
- Salt and pepper, to taste
- Fresh basil leaves, chopped, for garnish

Instructions:

1. Heat the olive oil in a large skillet or Dutch oven over medium heat.
2. Add the diced onion to the skillet and cook until softened, about 5 minutes.
3. Add the minced garlic to the skillet and cook for an additional minute, until fragrant.
4. Add the diced eggplant to the skillet and cook, stirring occasionally, until it starts to soften, about 5 minutes.
5. Add the diced zucchini and bell peppers to the skillet and cook for another 5 minutes, until they begin to soften.
6. Stir in the diced fresh tomatoes and crushed tomatoes, along with the dried thyme and dried oregano.
7. Season the ratatouille with salt and pepper to taste. Stir well to combine all the ingredients.
8. Reduce the heat to low and let the ratatouille simmer gently for about 20-25 minutes, stirring occasionally, until all the vegetables are tender and the flavors have melded together.
9. Taste the ratatouille and adjust the seasoning with salt and pepper, if needed.
10. Once the ratatouille is cooked to your liking, remove it from the heat and let it cool slightly.
11. Garnish the ratatouille with chopped fresh basil leaves just before serving.

12. Serve the fresh garden ratatouille warm or at room temperature, as a delicious side dish or main course.

Enjoy your homemade fresh garden ratatouille as a flavorful and satisfying dish that highlights the best of summer vegetables!

Grilled Pork Chops with Apple Chutney

Ingredients:

For the Pork Chops:

- 4 pork chops, about 2 cm thick
- Salt and pepper, to taste
- 2 tablespoons olive oil

For the Apple Chutney:

- 2 apples, peeled, cored, and diced
- 1/2 cup diced onion
- 1/4 cup apple cider vinegar
- 1/4 cup brown sugar
- 1/4 cup raisins or dried cranberries
- 1/2 teaspoon ground cinnamon
- 1/4 teaspoon ground ginger
- Pinch of salt
- Pinch of red pepper flakes (optional)

Instructions:

1. Preheat your grill to medium-high heat.
2. Season the pork chops with salt and pepper on both sides.
3. Drizzle the olive oil over the pork chops and rub it into the meat.
4. Place the pork chops on the preheated grill and cook for 4-5 minutes per side, or until they are cooked through and have nice grill marks. The internal temperature should reach 63°C (145°F). Cooking time may vary depending on the thickness of the pork chops.
5. While the pork chops are grilling, prepare the apple chutney. In a saucepan, combine the diced apples, diced onion, apple cider vinegar, brown sugar, raisins or dried cranberries, ground cinnamon, ground ginger, salt, and red pepper flakes (if using).

6. Bring the mixture to a simmer over medium heat. Reduce the heat to low and let the chutney cook for about 15-20 minutes, stirring occasionally, until the apples are soft and the mixture has thickened slightly.
7. Taste the apple chutney and adjust the seasoning if needed, adding more sugar or vinegar to balance the flavors.
8. Once the pork chops are cooked through, remove them from the grill and let them rest for a few minutes before serving.
9. Serve the grilled pork chops hot, topped with a generous spoonful of apple chutney.
10. Enjoy your delicious grilled pork chops with apple chutney as a flavorful and satisfying meal!

This dish pairs well with roasted vegetables, mashed potatoes, or a fresh salad.

Slow Cooker Beef Pot Roast

Ingredients:

- 1.5 kg beef chuck roast
- Salt and pepper, to taste
- 2 tablespoons olive oil
- 4 carrots, peeled and cut into chunks
- 4 potatoes, peeled and cut into chunks
- 2 onions, peeled and quartered
- 4 cloves garlic, minced
- 2 cups beef broth
- 1/4 cup soy sauce
- 2 tablespoons Worcestershire sauce
- 2 tablespoons tomato paste
- 2 teaspoons dried thyme
- 2 teaspoons dried rosemary
- 2 bay leaves
- 2 tablespoons cornstarch (optional, for thickening)
- 2 tablespoons water (optional, for thickening)
- Chopped fresh parsley, for garnish (optional)

Instructions:

1. Season the beef chuck roast generously with salt and pepper on all sides.
2. Heat the olive oil in a large skillet over medium-high heat. Add the seasoned beef chuck roast to the skillet and sear it on all sides until browned, about 3-4 minutes per side. Transfer the seared roast to the slow cooker.
3. Add the carrots, potatoes, onions, and minced garlic to the slow cooker, arranging them around the beef roast.
4. In a mixing bowl, whisk together the beef broth, soy sauce, Worcestershire sauce, tomato paste, dried thyme, dried rosemary, and bay leaves. Pour the mixture over the beef roast and vegetables in the slow cooker.
5. Cover the slow cooker with the lid and cook the beef pot roast on low heat for 8-10 hours, or on high heat for 4-5 hours, until the beef is tender and easily shreds with a fork.

6. Once the beef pot roast is cooked, carefully remove the beef roast and vegetables from the slow cooker and transfer them to a serving platter. Cover the platter loosely with aluminum foil to keep the roast warm.
7. If desired, thicken the cooking liquid in the slow cooker to make gravy. In a small bowl, mix together the cornstarch and water to make a slurry. Stir the slurry into the cooking liquid in the slow cooker. Cover and cook on high heat for an additional 15-20 minutes, or until the gravy has thickened.
8. Remove the bay leaves from the gravy and discard them.
9. Slice the beef roast against the grain into thick slices.
10. Serve the slow cooker beef pot roast and vegetables hot, drizzled with the gravy. Garnish with chopped fresh parsley, if desired.

Enjoy your homemade slow cooker beef pot roast as a comforting and satisfying meal!

Savory Sausage and Pepper Skillet

Ingredients:

- 500g Italian sausage, sliced into rounds
- 2 bell peppers, sliced (use a mix of colors for visual appeal)
- 1 onion, sliced
- 3 cloves garlic, minced
- 2 tablespoons olive oil
- 1 teaspoon Italian seasoning
- Salt and pepper, to taste
- Chopped fresh parsley, for garnish (optional)

Instructions:

1. Heat the olive oil in a large skillet over medium heat.
2. Add the sliced Italian sausage to the skillet and cook until browned and cooked through, about 5-7 minutes. Remove the cooked sausage from the skillet and set aside.
3. In the same skillet, add the sliced bell peppers and onion. Cook, stirring occasionally, until the vegetables are softened and slightly caramelized, about 5-7 minutes.
4. Add the minced garlic to the skillet and cook for an additional minute, until fragrant.
5. Return the cooked sausage to the skillet with the peppers and onions.
6. Season the sausage and pepper mixture with Italian seasoning, salt, and pepper to taste. Stir well to combine all the ingredients.
7. Continue to cook the sausage and pepper mixture for another 2-3 minutes, until heated through and the flavors have melded together.
8. Taste and adjust the seasoning with salt and pepper, if needed.
9. Once the sausage and peppers are cooked to your liking, remove the skillet from the heat.
10. Garnish the savory sausage and pepper skillet with chopped fresh parsley, if desired.
11. Serve the sausage and pepper skillet hot, either on its own or over cooked rice or pasta.

Enjoy your homemade savory sausage and pepper skillet as a delicious and satisfying meal!

Buttermilk Biscuits with Sausage Gravy

Ingredients:

For the Buttermilk Biscuits:

- 2 cups all-purpose flour
- 1 tablespoon baking powder
- 1/2 teaspoon baking soda
- 1/2 teaspoon salt
- 1/2 cup unsalted butter, cold and cut into small cubes
- 3/4 cup buttermilk

For the Sausage Gravy:

- 500g breakfast sausage (pork or turkey), casings removed
- 1/4 cup all-purpose flour
- 2 cups whole milk
- Salt and pepper, to taste

Instructions:

1. Preheat your oven to 220°C (425°F). Line a baking sheet with parchment paper.
2. In a large mixing bowl, whisk together the all-purpose flour, baking powder, baking soda, and salt.
3. Add the cold cubed butter to the flour mixture. Using a pastry cutter or your fingers, cut the butter into the flour until the mixture resembles coarse crumbs.
4. Make a well in the center of the flour mixture and pour in the buttermilk. Stir until the dough comes together and forms a soft ball.
5. Turn the dough out onto a lightly floured surface. Pat it into a rectangle about 1 inch thick.
6. Using a biscuit cutter or a glass, cut out biscuits from the dough. Place the biscuits on the prepared baking sheet, leaving a little space between each one.
7. Gently reroll any scraps of dough and cut out additional biscuits until all the dough is used up.

8. Bake the biscuits in the preheated oven for 12-15 minutes, or until they are golden brown on top.
9. While the biscuits are baking, prepare the sausage gravy. In a large skillet, cook the breakfast sausage over medium heat, breaking it up with a spoon, until it is browned and cooked through, about 8-10 minutes.
10. Sprinkle the cooked sausage with the all-purpose flour and stir well to coat. Cook for an additional 1-2 minutes to cook out the raw taste of the flour.
11. Gradually pour in the whole milk, stirring constantly, until the gravy thickens and comes to a simmer. Cook for another 2-3 minutes, stirring occasionally, until the gravy is smooth and thickened.
12. Season the sausage gravy with salt and pepper to taste.
13. Once the biscuits are done baking, remove them from the oven and let them cool slightly on the baking sheet.
14. Split the warm buttermilk biscuits in half and place them on serving plates. Spoon the hot sausage gravy over the biscuits.
15. Serve the buttermilk biscuits with sausage gravy hot, garnished with freshly ground black pepper if desired.

Enjoy your homemade buttermilk biscuits with sausage gravy as a delicious and comforting breakfast or brunch!

Farmhouse Macaroni and Cheese

Ingredients:

- 350g elbow macaroni
- 1/4 cup unsalted butter
- 1/4 cup all-purpose flour
- 2 cups whole milk
- 2 cups shredded sharp cheddar cheese
- 1 cup shredded mozzarella cheese
- 1/2 cup grated Parmesan cheese
- Salt and pepper, to taste
- 1/2 cup breadcrumbs (optional, for topping)
- Chopped fresh parsley, for garnish (optional)

Instructions:

1. Preheat your oven to 180°C (350°F). Grease a 9x13-inch baking dish with butter or cooking spray.
2. Cook the elbow macaroni according to the package instructions until al dente. Drain the cooked macaroni and set it aside.
3. In a large saucepan, melt the unsalted butter over medium heat. Once melted, whisk in the all-purpose flour to form a roux. Cook the roux for 1-2 minutes, stirring constantly, until it becomes golden brown and fragrant.
4. Gradually whisk in the whole milk, stirring constantly to prevent lumps from forming. Cook the sauce until it thickens and begins to bubble, about 5-7 minutes.
5. Once the sauce has thickened, remove the saucepan from the heat. Stir in the shredded sharp cheddar cheese, shredded mozzarella cheese, and grated Parmesan cheese until the cheeses are melted and the sauce is smooth.
6. Season the cheese sauce with salt and pepper to taste.
7. Add the cooked elbow macaroni to the cheese sauce, stirring until the macaroni is evenly coated with the cheese sauce.
8. Transfer the macaroni and cheese mixture to the prepared baking dish, spreading it out evenly.
9. If desired, sprinkle the breadcrumbs over the top of the macaroni and cheese for a crunchy topping.

10. Bake the farmhouse macaroni and cheese in the preheated oven for 20-25 minutes, or until the cheese is bubbly and the top is golden brown.
11. Once done, remove the baking dish from the oven and let the macaroni and cheese cool for a few minutes before serving.
12. Garnish the farmhouse macaroni and cheese with chopped fresh parsley, if desired.

Enjoy your homemade farmhouse macaroni and cheese as a comforting and satisfying meal!

Baked Beans with Bacon

Ingredients:

- 4 slices bacon, chopped
- 1 onion, finely chopped
- 2 cloves garlic, minced
- 2 cans (400g each) of navy beans or cannellini beans, drained and rinsed
- 1/4 cup ketchup
- 2 tablespoons brown sugar
- 1 tablespoon molasses
- 1 tablespoon Worcestershire sauce
- 1 teaspoon mustard powder
- Salt and pepper, to taste
- Chopped fresh parsley, for garnish (optional)

Instructions:

1. Preheat your oven to 180°C (350°F). Grease a baking dish with butter or cooking spray.
2. In a large skillet, cook the chopped bacon over medium heat until it is crispy and the fat has rendered, about 5-7 minutes.
3. Add the finely chopped onion to the skillet with the bacon and cook until the onion is soft and translucent, about 5 minutes.
4. Add the minced garlic to the skillet and cook for an additional minute, until fragrant.
5. Stir in the drained and rinsed navy beans or cannellini beans, along with the ketchup, brown sugar, molasses, Worcestershire sauce, mustard powder, salt, and pepper. Mix well to combine all the ingredients.
6. Transfer the bean mixture to the prepared baking dish, spreading it out evenly.
7. Cover the baking dish with aluminum foil and bake the beans in the preheated oven for 30 minutes.
8. After 30 minutes, remove the foil from the baking dish and continue to bake the beans for an additional 15-20 minutes, or until the sauce has thickened and the beans are bubbly.
9. Once done, remove the baked beans from the oven and let them cool for a few minutes before serving.

10. Garnish the baked beans with chopped fresh parsley, if desired.

Enjoy your homemade baked beans with bacon as a delicious and comforting side dish!

Lemon Herb Roasted Chicken

Ingredients:

- 1 whole chicken (about 1.5 to 2 kg), giblets removed
- 2 lemons, halved
- 4 cloves garlic, minced
- 2 tablespoons olive oil
- 2 tablespoons fresh herbs (such as rosemary, thyme, and parsley), chopped
- Salt and pepper, to taste
- Additional fresh herbs, for garnish (optional)

Instructions:

1. Preheat your oven to 200°C (400°F). Grease a roasting pan or baking dish with olive oil or cooking spray.
2. Rinse the whole chicken under cold water and pat it dry with paper towels. Place the chicken in the prepared roasting pan.
3. Rub the minced garlic all over the surface of the chicken, making sure to get it into the nooks and crannies.
4. Squeeze the juice of one lemon all over the chicken, then place the lemon halves inside the cavity of the chicken.
5. Drizzle the olive oil over the chicken, then sprinkle the chopped fresh herbs on top. Season the chicken generously with salt and pepper.
6. Cut the remaining lemon into slices and arrange them around the chicken in the roasting pan.
7. Roast the chicken in the preheated oven for 1 to 1.5 hours, or until the juices run clear when the thickest part of the thigh is pierced with a skewer or a meat thermometer inserted into the thickest part of the thigh registers 75°C (165°F).
8. If the skin starts to brown too quickly during roasting, you can tent the chicken with aluminum foil.
9. Once the chicken is cooked through and golden brown, remove it from the oven and let it rest for 10-15 minutes before carving.
10. Garnish the lemon herb roasted chicken with additional fresh herbs, if desired.
11. Carve the roasted chicken into serving pieces and serve hot, accompanied by your favorite sides such as roasted vegetables, mashed potatoes, or a fresh salad.

Enjoy your homemade lemon herb roasted chicken as a delicious and satisfying meal!

Corn Chowder with Bacon

Ingredients:

- 6 slices bacon, chopped
- 1 onion, diced
- 2 cloves garlic, minced
- 2 potatoes, peeled and diced
- 4 cups corn kernels (fresh, frozen, or canned)
- 4 cups chicken or vegetable broth
- 1 cup heavy cream
- 2 tablespoons all-purpose flour
- Salt and pepper, to taste
- Chopped fresh chives, for garnish (optional)

Instructions:

1. In a large pot or Dutch oven, cook the chopped bacon over medium heat until it is crispy and the fat has rendered, about 5-7 minutes.
2. Remove the cooked bacon from the pot and set it aside on a plate lined with paper towels to drain. Leave the bacon fat in the pot.
3. Add the diced onion to the pot with the bacon fat and cook until the onion is soft and translucent, about 5 minutes.
4. Add the minced garlic to the pot and cook for an additional minute, until fragrant.
5. Stir in the diced potatoes and corn kernels, then pour in the chicken or vegetable broth.
6. Bring the mixture to a simmer and let it cook for about 15-20 minutes, or until the potatoes are tender.
7. In a small bowl, whisk together the heavy cream and all-purpose flour until smooth. Pour the mixture into the pot, stirring constantly, until the soup thickens slightly.
8. Season the corn chowder with salt and pepper to taste.
9. Ladle the corn chowder into bowls and garnish each serving with the cooked bacon and chopped fresh chives, if desired.
10. Serve the corn chowder hot, accompanied by crusty bread or oyster crackers.

Enjoy your homemade corn chowder with bacon as a delicious and satisfying meal!

Zucchini and Tomato Frittata

Ingredients:

- 6 large eggs
- 1/4 cup milk or heavy cream
- Salt and pepper, to taste
- 2 tablespoons olive oil
- 1 small onion, diced
- 2 cloves garlic, minced
- 1 medium zucchini, thinly sliced
- 1 large tomato, diced
- 1/2 cup grated Parmesan cheese
- 2 tablespoons chopped fresh basil or parsley (optional)
- Additional grated Parmesan cheese, for serving (optional)

Instructions:

1. Preheat your oven to 200°C (400°F).
2. In a mixing bowl, whisk together the eggs, milk or heavy cream, salt, and pepper until well combined. Set aside.
3. Heat the olive oil in an oven-safe skillet (preferably non-stick) over medium heat.
4. Add the diced onion to the skillet and cook until it is soft and translucent, about 5 minutes.
5. Add the minced garlic to the skillet and cook for an additional minute, until fragrant.
6. Add the thinly sliced zucchini to the skillet and cook, stirring occasionally, until it is tender and lightly browned, about 5-7 minutes.
7. Stir in the diced tomato and cook for another 2-3 minutes, until the tomato is heated through.
8. Spread the cooked vegetables evenly in the skillet and sprinkle the grated Parmesan cheese over the top.
9. Pour the egg mixture evenly over the vegetables and cheese in the skillet.
10. Cook the frittata on the stovetop for 3-4 minutes, until the edges are set but the center is still slightly runny.
11. Transfer the skillet to the preheated oven and bake the frittata for 8-10 minutes, or until it is set and golden brown on top.

12. Once done, remove the skillet from the oven and let the frittata cool for a few minutes before slicing.
13. Sprinkle the chopped fresh basil or parsley over the top of the frittata, if desired. Serve hot, accompanied by additional grated Parmesan cheese if desired.

Enjoy your homemade zucchini and tomato frittata as a delicious and nutritious meal!

Honey Glazed Carrots

Ingredients:

- 500g carrots, peeled and sliced into rounds or sticks
- 2 tablespoons unsalted butter
- 2 tablespoons honey
- Salt and pepper, to taste
- Chopped fresh parsley, for garnish (optional)

Instructions:

1. Bring a pot of water to a boil over high heat. Add the sliced carrots to the boiling water and cook for about 5-7 minutes, or until they are tender but still slightly crisp.
2. Drain the cooked carrots and set them aside.
3. In a large skillet, melt the unsalted butter over medium heat.
4. Add the cooked carrots to the skillet with the melted butter.
5. Drizzle the honey over the carrots and stir well to coat them evenly.
6. Cook the carrots in the skillet, stirring occasionally, for about 3-4 minutes, or until they are glazed and heated through.
7. Season the honey glazed carrots with salt and pepper to taste.
8. Once done, remove the skillet from the heat and transfer the honey glazed carrots to a serving dish.
9. Garnish the honey glazed carrots with chopped fresh parsley, if desired.
10. Serve the honey glazed carrots hot as a delicious and colorful side dish.

Enjoy your homemade honey glazed carrots as a sweet and savory accompaniment to any meal!

Beef and Vegetable Stir-Fry

Ingredients:

- 500g beef steak (such as sirloin or flank), thinly sliced
- 2 tablespoons soy sauce
- 1 tablespoon oyster sauce
- 1 tablespoon hoisin sauce
- 1 tablespoon cornstarch
- 2 tablespoons vegetable oil, divided
- 2 cloves garlic, minced
- 1 onion, sliced
- 1 bell pepper, sliced
- 1 carrot, julienned
- 1 cup broccoli florets
- 1 cup snap peas
- Salt and pepper, to taste
- Cooked rice or noodles, for serving

Instructions:

1. In a bowl, combine the thinly sliced beef with the soy sauce, oyster sauce, hoisin sauce, and cornstarch. Toss to coat the beef evenly and let it marinate for 15-20 minutes.
2. Heat 1 tablespoon of vegetable oil in a large skillet or wok over high heat.
3. Add the marinated beef to the hot skillet and stir-fry for 2-3 minutes, or until it is browned and cooked through. Remove the beef from the skillet and set it aside on a plate.
4. In the same skillet, add the remaining tablespoon of vegetable oil.
5. Add the minced garlic to the skillet and cook for 30 seconds, until fragrant.
6. Add the sliced onion, bell pepper, julienned carrot, broccoli florets, and snap peas to the skillet. Stir-fry for 4-5 minutes, or until the vegetables are crisp-tender.
7. Return the cooked beef to the skillet with the vegetables. Stir well to combine all the ingredients.
8. Season the beef and vegetable stir-fry with salt and pepper to taste.
9. Once everything is heated through, remove the skillet from the heat.
10. Serve the beef and vegetable stir-fry hot over cooked rice or noodles.

Enjoy your homemade beef and vegetable stir-fry as a flavorful and satisfying meal!

Apple Crisp with Oats and Cinnamon

Ingredients:

For the Apple Filling:

- 6 medium apples, peeled, cored, and sliced
- 1/4 cup granulated sugar
- 1 tablespoon all-purpose flour
- 1 teaspoon ground cinnamon
- 1/4 teaspoon ground nutmeg
- 1 tablespoon lemon juice

For the Oat Topping:

- 1 cup old-fashioned oats
- 1/2 cup all-purpose flour
- 1/2 cup brown sugar
- 1/2 teaspoon ground cinnamon
- 1/4 teaspoon salt
- 1/2 cup unsalted butter, melted

Instructions:

1. Preheat your oven to 180°C (350°F). Grease a 9x9-inch baking dish with butter or cooking spray.
2. In a large mixing bowl, combine the sliced apples, granulated sugar, all-purpose flour, ground cinnamon, ground nutmeg, and lemon juice. Toss the ingredients together until the apples are evenly coated.
3. Transfer the apple mixture to the prepared baking dish, spreading it out evenly.
4. In a separate mixing bowl, combine the old-fashioned oats, all-purpose flour, brown sugar, ground cinnamon, and salt. Stir to combine.
5. Pour the melted butter over the oat mixture and stir until the ingredients are well combined and crumbly.
6. Sprinkle the oat topping evenly over the apple mixture in the baking dish.

7. Bake the apple crisp in the preheated oven for 40-45 minutes, or until the topping is golden brown and the apples are tender and bubbly.
8. Once done, remove the apple crisp from the oven and let it cool for a few minutes before serving.
9. Serve the apple crisp warm, optionally with a scoop of vanilla ice cream or a dollop of whipped cream.

Enjoy your homemade apple crisp with oats and cinnamon as a delicious and comforting dessert!

Farmhouse Meatloaf with Tomato Glaze

Ingredients:

For the Meatloaf:

- 500g ground beef (or a mixture of beef and pork)
- 1 onion, finely chopped
- 2 cloves garlic, minced
- 1 cup breadcrumbs
- 1/4 cup milk
- 1/4 cup ketchup
- 1 tablespoon Worcestershire sauce
- 1 teaspoon dried thyme
- 1 teaspoon dried oregano
- 1/2 teaspoon salt
- 1/4 teaspoon black pepper
- 1 egg, beaten

For the Tomato Glaze:

- 1/2 cup ketchup
- 2 tablespoons brown sugar
- 1 tablespoon Dijon mustard
- 1 tablespoon apple cider vinegar

Instructions:

1. Preheat your oven to 180°C (350°F). Grease a loaf pan with butter or cooking spray.
2. In a large mixing bowl, combine the ground beef, finely chopped onion, minced garlic, breadcrumbs, milk, ketchup, Worcestershire sauce, dried thyme, dried oregano, salt, black pepper, and beaten egg. Use your hands or a spoon to mix everything together until well combined.
3. Transfer the meatloaf mixture to the prepared loaf pan, pressing it down evenly.

4. In a small bowl, mix together the ketchup, brown sugar, Dijon mustard, and apple cider vinegar to make the tomato glaze.
5. Spread the tomato glaze evenly over the top of the meatloaf in the loaf pan.
6. Bake the meatloaf in the preheated oven for 50-60 minutes, or until it is cooked through and the top is caramelized and glazed.
7. Once done, remove the meatloaf from the oven and let it rest for a few minutes before slicing.
8. Serve the farmhouse meatloaf with tomato glaze hot, accompanied by mashed potatoes, steamed vegetables, or your favorite side dishes.

Enjoy your homemade farmhouse meatloaf with tomato glaze as a comforting and satisfying meal!

Cucumber and Tomato Salad with Balsamic Vinaigrette

Ingredients:

For the Salad:

- 2 cucumbers, thinly sliced
- 4 tomatoes, diced
- 1/2 red onion, thinly sliced
- 1/4 cup fresh basil leaves, torn
- Salt and pepper, to taste

For the Balsamic Vinaigrette:

- 1/4 cup balsamic vinegar
- 1/4 cup extra virgin olive oil
- 1 tablespoon Dijon mustard
- 1 teaspoon honey (optional)
- 1 clove garlic, minced
- Salt and pepper, to taste

Instructions:

1. In a large mixing bowl, combine the thinly sliced cucumbers, diced tomatoes, thinly sliced red onion, and torn basil leaves. Toss the ingredients together until well combined.
2. In a separate small bowl, whisk together the balsamic vinegar, extra virgin olive oil, Dijon mustard, honey (if using), minced garlic, salt, and pepper to make the balsamic vinaigrette.
3. Pour the balsamic vinaigrette over the cucumber and tomato salad in the large mixing bowl. Toss well to coat all the ingredients evenly with the dressing.
4. Season the salad with additional salt and pepper to taste, if needed.
5. Let the cucumber and tomato salad marinate in the refrigerator for at least 15-20 minutes before serving to allow the flavors to meld together.
6. Once marinated, give the salad a final toss, then transfer it to a serving bowl or platter.

7. Garnish the cucumber and tomato salad with additional torn basil leaves, if desired.
8. Serve the cucumber and tomato salad with balsamic vinaigrette chilled or at room temperature as a refreshing side dish.

Enjoy your homemade cucumber and tomato salad with balsamic vinaigrette as a delicious and healthy addition to any meal!

Creamy Chicken and Mushroom Pasta

Ingredients:

- 300g pasta (such as fettuccine or penne)
- 2 chicken breasts, sliced into thin strips
- Salt and pepper, to taste
- 2 tablespoons olive oil
- 250g mushrooms, sliced
- 2 cloves garlic, minced
- 1 cup chicken broth
- 1 cup heavy cream
- 1/2 cup grated Parmesan cheese
- 2 tablespoons chopped fresh parsley
- Additional grated Parmesan cheese, for serving (optional)

Instructions:

1. Cook the pasta according to the package instructions until al dente. Drain and set aside.
2. Season the sliced chicken breasts with salt and pepper to taste.
3. Heat one tablespoon of olive oil in a large skillet over medium-high heat. Add the seasoned chicken strips to the skillet and cook until they are browned and cooked through, about 5-6 minutes per side. Once cooked, transfer the chicken to a plate and set aside.
4. In the same skillet, add the remaining tablespoon of olive oil. Add the sliced mushrooms to the skillet and cook until they are golden brown and tender, about 5-6 minutes.
5. Add the minced garlic to the skillet with the mushrooms and cook for an additional minute, until fragrant.
6. Pour the chicken broth into the skillet and bring it to a simmer. Let it cook for 2-3 minutes to reduce slightly.
7. Stir in the heavy cream and grated Parmesan cheese. Cook, stirring constantly, until the sauce thickens slightly, about 3-4 minutes.
8. Return the cooked chicken strips to the skillet and stir to coat them in the creamy mushroom sauce.
9. Add the cooked pasta to the skillet and toss everything together until the pasta is evenly coated in the sauce.

10. Remove the skillet from the heat and stir in the chopped fresh parsley.
11. Serve the creamy chicken and mushroom pasta hot, garnished with additional grated Parmesan cheese if desired.

Enjoy your homemade creamy chicken and mushroom pasta as a delicious and comforting meal!

Roasted Root Vegetables with Thyme

Ingredients:

- 2 pounds mixed root vegetables (such as carrots, parsnips, potatoes, sweet potatoes, turnips, etc.), peeled and cut into chunks
- 2 tablespoons olive oil
- 2-3 cloves garlic, minced
- 2-3 teaspoons fresh thyme leaves (or 1 teaspoon dried thyme)
- Salt and pepper to taste

Instructions:

1. Preheat your oven to 400°F (200°C).
2. In a large bowl, toss the chopped root vegetables with olive oil, minced garlic, fresh thyme leaves, salt, and pepper until evenly coated.
3. Spread the vegetables out in a single layer on a baking sheet lined with parchment paper or aluminum foil.
4. Roast in the preheated oven for about 30-40 minutes, or until the vegetables are tender and golden brown, stirring halfway through to ensure even cooking.
5. Once roasted, remove from the oven and serve hot.

Feel free to customize this recipe based on your preferences. You can add other herbs like rosemary or sage for extra flavor, or even drizzle some balsamic glaze over the roasted vegetables before serving for a touch of sweetness. Enjoy your delicious roasted root vegetables with thyme!

Farm-Fresh Strawberry Shortcake

Ingredients:

For the Shortcakes:

- 2 cups all-purpose flour
- 1/4 cup granulated sugar
- 1 tablespoon baking powder
- 1/2 teaspoon salt
- 1/2 cup cold unsalted butter, cut into small pieces
- 3/4 cup cold heavy cream
- 1 teaspoon vanilla extract

For the Strawberry Filling:

- 1 1/2 pounds fresh strawberries, hulled and sliced
- 1/4 cup granulated sugar (adjust according to the sweetness of your strawberries)
- 1 tablespoon lemon juice
- Additional sugar for macerating the strawberries (optional)

For the Whipped Cream:

- 1 cup cold heavy cream
- 2 tablespoons powdered sugar
- 1 teaspoon vanilla extract

Instructions:

Shortcakes:

1. Preheat your oven to 425°F (220°C). Line a baking sheet with parchment paper.
2. In a large mixing bowl, whisk together the flour, sugar, baking powder, and salt.
3. Add the cold butter pieces to the flour mixture. Using a pastry cutter or your fingers, work the butter into the flour until the mixture resembles coarse crumbs.
4. In a separate bowl, mix together the cold heavy cream and vanilla extract.
5. Pour the cream mixture into the flour mixture and stir until just combined. Do not overmix.

6. Turn the dough out onto a lightly floured surface and gently pat it into a circle about 1-inch thick. Use a biscuit cutter or a glass to cut out rounds of dough.
7. Place the dough rounds onto the prepared baking sheet and bake for 12-15 minutes, or until golden brown. Remove from the oven and let cool slightly.

Strawberry Filling:

1. In a bowl, combine the sliced strawberries, granulated sugar, and lemon juice. If your strawberries are not very sweet, you can add a bit more sugar to taste.
2. Let the strawberries sit at room temperature for about 30 minutes to macerate, allowing the sugar to draw out the juices and create a syrup.

Whipped Cream:

1. In a chilled mixing bowl, beat the cold heavy cream, powdered sugar, and vanilla extract together until stiff peaks form.

Assembly:

1. Once the shortcakes have cooled slightly, split them in half horizontally.
2. Place the bottom halves of the shortcakes on serving plates. Spoon a generous amount of macerated strawberries over each bottom half.
3. Top the strawberries with a dollop of whipped cream.
4. Place the top halves of the shortcakes over the whipped cream.
5. Garnish with additional whipped cream and whole strawberries if desired.
6. Serve immediately and enjoy your farm-fresh strawberry shortcake!

This dessert is best enjoyed fresh, but you can store any leftovers in an airtight container in the refrigerator for a day or two.

Slow Cooker Pulled Pork Sandwiches

Ingredients:

For the Pulled Pork:

- 3-4 pounds pork shoulder (also known as pork butt), trimmed of excess fat
- 1 tablespoon brown sugar
- 1 tablespoon paprika
- 1 tablespoon garlic powder
- 1 tablespoon onion powder
- 1 teaspoon cumin
- 1 teaspoon chili powder
- Salt and black pepper to taste
- 1 cup chicken broth or apple juice
- 1/2 cup barbecue sauce (plus extra for serving)

For Serving:

- Hamburger buns or sandwich rolls
- Coleslaw (optional, for topping)

Instructions:

1. In a small bowl, mix together the brown sugar, paprika, garlic powder, onion powder, cumin, chili powder, salt, and black pepper to create a dry rub.
2. Rub the dry rub all over the pork shoulder, covering it evenly.
3. Place the pork shoulder in the slow cooker.
4. Pour the chicken broth or apple juice over the pork shoulder.
5. Cover the slow cooker and cook on low for 8-10 hours or on high for 4-6 hours, until the pork is very tender and falls apart easily.
6. Once the pork is cooked, remove it from the slow cooker and shred it using two forks. Discard any excess fat.
7. Place the shredded pork back into the slow cooker and stir in the barbecue sauce. Cook for an additional 30 minutes on low to allow the flavors to meld.
8. To serve, spoon the pulled pork onto hamburger buns or sandwich rolls. Top with coleslaw if desired, and drizzle with extra barbecue sauce.
9. Serve hot and enjoy your delicious slow cooker pulled pork sandwiches!

You can customize this recipe by adjusting the seasonings in the dry rub or using your favorite barbecue sauce. These sandwiches pair well with coleslaw, pickles, or a side of potato salad.

Garlic Herb Roasted Potatoes

Ingredients:

- 2 pounds baby potatoes, halved or quartered if large
- 3 tablespoons olive oil
- 4 cloves garlic, minced
- 1 teaspoon dried thyme (or 1 tablespoon fresh thyme leaves)
- 1 teaspoon dried rosemary (or 1 tablespoon fresh rosemary, chopped)
- 1 teaspoon dried parsley (or 1 tablespoon fresh parsley, chopped)
- Salt and black pepper to taste
- Optional: grated Parmesan cheese for serving

Instructions:

1. Preheat your oven to 400°F (200°C). Line a baking sheet with parchment paper or aluminum foil for easy cleanup.
2. In a large bowl, combine the halved baby potatoes, olive oil, minced garlic, dried thyme, dried rosemary, dried parsley, salt, and black pepper. Toss until the potatoes are evenly coated with the seasonings.
3. Spread the seasoned potatoes out in a single layer on the prepared baking sheet.
4. Roast in the preheated oven for about 30-35 minutes, or until the potatoes are golden brown and crispy on the outside, and tender on the inside. Stir the potatoes halfway through the cooking time to ensure even browning.
5. Once the potatoes are roasted to your desired level of crispiness, remove them from the oven.
6. Optional: Sprinkle the roasted potatoes with grated Parmesan cheese while they're still hot for an extra burst of flavor.
7. Transfer the roasted potatoes to a serving dish and garnish with additional fresh herbs if desired.
8. Serve hot as a side dish alongside your favorite main course. Enjoy your delicious garlic herb roasted potatoes!

Feel free to customize this recipe by adding other herbs or spices, such as oregano or smoked paprika, to suit your taste preferences.

Grilled Vegetable Platter with Herb Butter

Ingredients:

For the Herb Butter:

- 1/2 cup (1 stick) unsalted butter, softened
- 2 tablespoons finely chopped fresh herbs (such as parsley, basil, thyme, rosemary, or a combination)
- 2 cloves garlic, minced
- Salt and black pepper to taste

For the Grilled Vegetables:

- Assorted vegetables, such as:
    - Zucchini, sliced lengthwise
    - Yellow squash, sliced lengthwise
    - Bell peppers, halved and seeded
    - Red onions, sliced into thick rounds
    - Eggplant, sliced into rounds
    - Asparagus spears, trimmed
    - Cherry tomatoes (you can thread these onto skewers for easy grilling)
- Olive oil
- Salt and black pepper to taste
- Additional fresh herbs for garnish (optional)

Instructions:

Herb Butter:

1. In a small bowl, combine the softened butter, finely chopped fresh herbs, minced garlic, salt, and black pepper. Mix until well combined.
2. Transfer the herb butter onto a sheet of plastic wrap or parchment paper. Roll it into a log shape and twist the ends to seal.
3. Place the herb butter in the refrigerator to chill and firm up while you prepare the vegetables.

Grilled Vegetables:

1. Preheat your grill to medium-high heat.
2. Prepare the vegetables by slicing or trimming them as needed. If using wooden skewers for cherry tomatoes, soak them in water for about 30 minutes before grilling to prevent burning.
3. Drizzle the vegetables with olive oil and season with salt and black pepper. Toss to coat evenly.
4. Place the vegetables on the preheated grill. Cook, turning occasionally, until they are tender and charred in spots, about 8-10 minutes depending on the vegetable. Cook cherry tomatoes on skewers until they are softened and slightly blistered, about 4-5 minutes.
5. Once the vegetables are cooked to your liking, transfer them to a serving platter.
6. Remove the herb butter from the refrigerator and slice it into discs.
7. Arrange the herb butter discs over the hot grilled vegetables, allowing them to melt and infuse the vegetables with flavor.
8. Garnish the platter with additional fresh herbs if desired.
9. Serve the grilled vegetable platter immediately as a side dish or appetizer, and enjoy!

This dish is not only delicious but also colorful and visually appealing, making it perfect for entertaining. Feel free to customize the selection of vegetables based on what's in season or your personal preferences.

Classic Farmhouse Pancakes with Maple Syrup

Ingredients:

- 1 1/2 cups all-purpose flour
- 3 1/2 teaspoons baking powder
- 1 teaspoon salt
- 1 tablespoon granulated sugar
- 1 1/4 cups milk
- 1 large egg
- 3 tablespoons unsalted butter, melted
- Maple syrup, for serving
- Optional toppings: butter, fresh berries, sliced bananas, whipped cream

Instructions:

1. In a large mixing bowl, sift together the all-purpose flour, baking powder, salt, and granulated sugar. This helps to ensure that your pancakes are light and fluffy.
2. In a separate bowl, whisk together the milk and egg until well combined.
3. Pour the melted butter into the milk and egg mixture and whisk until incorporated.
4. Make a well in the center of the dry ingredients and pour the wet ingredients into the well.
5. Stir the wet and dry ingredients together until just combined. Be careful not to overmix; a few lumps in the batter are okay.
6. Heat a lightly greased griddle or non-stick skillet over medium heat. You can test if the pan is hot enough by sprinkling a few drops of water onto the surface; if they sizzle and evaporate, it's ready.
7. Pour about 1/4 cup of batter onto the hot griddle for each pancake. Cook until bubbles form on the surface of the pancake and the edges begin to look set, about 2-3 minutes.
8. Flip the pancakes with a spatula and cook for an additional 1-2 minutes, or until golden brown and cooked through.
9. Transfer the cooked pancakes to a plate and keep warm while you cook the remaining batter. You may need to adjust the heat of the griddle or skillet as you cook to prevent burning.
10. Serve the pancakes hot, stacked high, with a generous drizzle of maple syrup over the top. Add any optional toppings you desire, such as butter, fresh berries, sliced bananas, or whipped cream.

11. Enjoy your classic farmhouse pancakes with maple syrup for a delicious and satisfying breakfast!

Feel free to customize this recipe by adding vanilla extract or spices like cinnamon or nutmeg to the batter for extra flavor. You can also use whole wheat flour or substitute some of the milk with buttermilk for a different texture and taste.

Chicken and Rice Casserole

Ingredients:

- 1 1/2 cups long-grain white rice
- 1 lb boneless, skinless chicken breasts or thighs, cut into bite-sized pieces
- 1 tablespoon olive oil
- 1 medium onion, chopped
- 2 cloves garlic, minced
- 1 cup sliced mushrooms (optional)
- 1 (10.5 oz) can condensed cream of chicken soup
- 1 (10.5 oz) can condensed cream of mushroom soup
- 2 cups chicken broth
- 1/2 cup milk or cream
- 1 teaspoon dried thyme
- 1 teaspoon dried parsley
- Salt and black pepper to taste
- 1 cup frozen peas (optional)
- 1 cup shredded cheddar cheese

Instructions:

1. Preheat your oven to 375°F (190°C). Grease a 9x13 inch baking dish.
2. In a large skillet, heat the olive oil over medium heat. Add the chopped onion and cook until softened, about 5 minutes. Add the minced garlic and cook for an additional 1 minute.
3. Add the chicken pieces to the skillet and cook until browned on all sides, about 5-7 minutes.
4. Stir in the sliced mushrooms (if using) and cook for another 3-4 minutes, until they start to soften.
5. In a large mixing bowl, combine the condensed cream of chicken soup, condensed cream of mushroom soup, chicken broth, milk or cream, dried thyme, dried parsley, salt, and black pepper. Mix until well combined.
6. Spread the uncooked rice evenly over the bottom of the prepared baking dish.
7. Layer the cooked chicken and onion mixture over the rice.
8. If using frozen peas, sprinkle them over the chicken layer.
9. Pour the soup mixture evenly over the top of the chicken and rice layers.
10. Cover the baking dish with aluminum foil and bake in the preheated oven for 45 minutes.

11. After 45 minutes, remove the foil and sprinkle the shredded cheddar cheese over the top of the casserole.
12. Return the uncovered casserole to the oven and bake for an additional 15-20 minutes, or until the cheese is melted and bubbly, and the rice is cooked through.
13. Once done, remove from the oven and let it rest for a few minutes before serving.
14. Serve hot and enjoy your delicious chicken and rice casserole!

Feel free to customize this recipe by adding other vegetables like carrots, broccoli, or bell peppers, or by using different herbs and spices to suit your taste preferences.

Fresh Berry Cobbler

Ingredients:

For the Berry Filling:

- 4 cups fresh mixed berries (such as strawberries, blueberries, raspberries, blackberries)
- 1/2 cup granulated sugar (adjust based on the sweetness of the berries)
- 2 tablespoons cornstarch
- 1 tablespoon lemon juice
- Zest of 1 lemon
- 1 teaspoon vanilla extract

For the Cobbler Topping:

- 1 cup all-purpose flour
- 1/4 cup granulated sugar
- 1 1/2 teaspoons baking powder
- 1/4 teaspoon salt
- 6 tablespoons unsalted butter, cold and cut into small pieces
- 1/4 cup milk
- 1 large egg
- 1 teaspoon vanilla extract

For Serving (optional):

- Vanilla ice cream or whipped cream

Instructions:

1. Preheat your oven to 375°F (190°C). Grease a 9x9 inch baking dish or a similar-sized ovenproof dish.
2. In a large bowl, gently toss together the mixed berries, granulated sugar, cornstarch, lemon juice, lemon zest, and vanilla extract until the berries are coated evenly. Transfer the berry mixture to the prepared baking dish, spreading it out evenly.
3. In another bowl, whisk together the flour, granulated sugar, baking powder, and salt.

4. Cut in the cold butter pieces using a pastry cutter or your fingers until the mixture resembles coarse crumbs.
5. In a small bowl, whisk together the milk, egg, and vanilla extract.
6. Pour the milk mixture into the flour mixture and stir until just combined. Do not overmix; it's okay if the batter is slightly lumpy.
7. Drop spoonfuls of the batter evenly over the top of the berry mixture in the baking dish, covering it as much as possible.
8. Bake in the preheated oven for 35-40 minutes, or until the cobbler topping is golden brown and the berry filling is bubbly.
9. Remove from the oven and let the cobbler cool for a few minutes before serving.
10. Serve warm, optionally topped with vanilla ice cream or whipped cream.
11. Enjoy your delicious fresh berry cobbler!

Feel free to adjust the type and amount of berries used based on what's in season or your personal preference. You can also add a sprinkle of cinnamon or nutmeg to the berry filling for extra flavor.

Skillet Cornbread with Jalapenos and Cheddar

Ingredients:

- 1 cup cornmeal
- 1 cup all-purpose flour
- 1 tablespoon baking powder
- 1 teaspoon salt
- 1/4 cup granulated sugar (optional, for a sweeter cornbread)
- 1 cup shredded cheddar cheese
- 2 jalapeno peppers, seeded and finely diced
- 1 cup buttermilk
- 1/2 cup unsalted butter, melted
- 2 large eggs

Instructions:

1. Preheat your oven to 400°F (200°C). Place a 10-inch cast iron skillet in the oven to heat while you prepare the batter.
2. In a large mixing bowl, whisk together the cornmeal, all-purpose flour, baking powder, salt, and granulated sugar (if using).
3. Stir in the shredded cheddar cheese and diced jalapenos until evenly distributed throughout the dry ingredients.
4. In a separate bowl, whisk together the buttermilk, melted butter, and eggs until well combined.
5. Pour the wet ingredients into the dry ingredients and stir until just combined. Be careful not to overmix; a few lumps in the batter are okay.
6. Carefully remove the hot skillet from the oven and pour the batter into the skillet, spreading it out evenly.
7. Return the skillet to the oven and bake for 20-25 minutes, or until the cornbread is golden brown on top and a toothpick inserted into the center comes out clean.
8. Once done, remove the skillet from the oven and let the cornbread cool for a few minutes before slicing and serving.
9. Serve the skillet cornbread warm as a side dish or snack.
10. Enjoy your delicious skillet cornbread with jalapenos and cheddar!

This cornbread pairs well with chili, soups, barbecue, or simply on its own with a dollop of butter. Adjust the amount of jalapenos according to your desired level of spiciness.

Spinach and Cheese Stuffed Chicken Breast

Ingredients:

- 4 boneless, skinless chicken breasts
- Salt and black pepper, to taste
- 1 tablespoon olive oil
- 2 cloves garlic, minced
- 4 cups fresh spinach leaves, chopped
- 1 cup shredded mozzarella cheese
- 1/4 cup grated Parmesan cheese
- 1/4 teaspoon red pepper flakes (optional, for a bit of heat)
- 1/2 teaspoon dried oregano
- 1/2 teaspoon dried basil
- 1/4 cup sun-dried tomatoes, chopped (optional)
- Toothpicks or kitchen twine, for securing the chicken breasts

Instructions:

1. Preheat your oven to 375°F (190°C).
2. Place each chicken breast between two sheets of plastic wrap or parchment paper. Use a meat mallet or rolling pin to pound the chicken to an even thickness of about 1/4 inch. This will make it easier to stuff and roll.
3. Season both sides of each chicken breast with salt and black pepper.
4. In a large skillet, heat the olive oil over medium heat. Add the minced garlic and cook for about 1 minute, until fragrant.
5. Add the chopped spinach to the skillet and cook, stirring frequently, until wilted, about 2-3 minutes. Remove from heat and let cool slightly.
6. In a mixing bowl, combine the cooked spinach, shredded mozzarella cheese, grated Parmesan cheese, red pepper flakes (if using), dried oregano, dried basil, and chopped sun-dried tomatoes (if using). Mix well to combine.
7. Place a portion of the spinach and cheese mixture onto one half of each chicken breast, leaving a small border around the edges. Be careful not to overfill.
8. Fold the other half of the chicken breast over the filling to enclose it. Secure the edges with toothpicks or tie with kitchen twine to hold the stuffed chicken breasts together.
9. Place the stuffed chicken breasts in a baking dish sprayed with cooking spray or lined with parchment paper.

10. Bake in the preheated oven for 25-30 minutes, or until the chicken is cooked through and the internal temperature reaches 165°F (75°C).
11. Once done, remove the toothpicks or twine from the chicken breasts.
12. Serve the spinach and cheese stuffed chicken breasts hot, garnished with fresh herbs if desired.
13. Enjoy your delicious stuffed chicken breasts as a main course alongside your favorite side dishes!

Feel free to customize this recipe by using different types of cheese or adding other ingredients to the stuffing mixture, such as cooked bacon, mushrooms, or artichoke hearts.

Farmhouse Chili with Beans and Cornbread Muffins

Farmhouse Chili with Beans:

Ingredients:

- 1 tablespoon olive oil
- 1 large onion, chopped
- 3 cloves garlic, minced
- 1 bell pepper, chopped (any color)
- 1 lb ground beef (or ground turkey)
- 1 can (14 oz) diced tomatoes
- 1 can (15 oz) kidney beans, drained and rinsed
- 1 can (15 oz) black beans, drained and rinsed
- 1 can (15 oz) corn kernels, drained
- 2 tablespoons tomato paste
- 2 cups beef or vegetable broth
- 2 tablespoons chili powder
- 1 tablespoon ground cumin
- 1 teaspoon paprika
- Salt and black pepper to taste
- Optional toppings: shredded cheese, chopped green onions, sour cream, avocado slices, cilantro

Instructions:

1. Heat olive oil in a large pot or Dutch oven over medium heat. Add chopped onion, minced garlic, and bell pepper. Cook until softened, about 5 minutes.
2. Add ground beef (or turkey) to the pot. Cook, breaking it apart with a spoon, until browned and cooked through.
3. Stir in diced tomatoes, kidney beans, black beans, corn kernels, tomato paste, broth, chili powder, cumin, paprika, salt, and black pepper.
4. Bring the chili to a simmer, then reduce heat to low. Cover and let it simmer for about 30 minutes to allow the flavors to meld together.
5. Taste and adjust seasoning if needed. If the chili is too thick, you can add more broth or water to reach your desired consistency.
6. Serve hot, garnished with your favorite toppings.

Cornbread Muffins:

Ingredients:

- 1 cup cornmeal
- 1 cup all-purpose flour
- 1/4 cup granulated sugar
- 1 tablespoon baking powder
- 1/2 teaspoon salt
- 1 cup milk
- 1/4 cup unsalted butter, melted
- 1 large egg

Instructions:

1. Preheat your oven to 400°F (200°C). Grease a muffin tin or line with paper liners.
2. In a large bowl, whisk together cornmeal, flour, sugar, baking powder, and salt.
3. In another bowl, whisk together milk, melted butter, and egg.
4. Pour the wet ingredients into the dry ingredients and stir until just combined. Do not overmix; it's okay if the batter is slightly lumpy.
5. Divide the batter evenly among the muffin cups, filling each about two-thirds full.
6. Bake in the preheated oven for 15-18 minutes, or until the muffins are golden brown and a toothpick inserted into the center comes out clean.
7. Remove from the oven and let the muffins cool in the pan for a few minutes before transferring them to a wire rack to cool completely.

Serve the warm chili alongside the freshly baked cornbread muffins for a comforting and delicious meal. Enjoy!

Grilled Corn on the Cob with Chili Lime Butter

Ingredients:

For the Chili Lime Butter:

- 1/2 cup (1 stick) unsalted butter, softened
- Zest of 1 lime
- 1 tablespoon lime juice
- 1 teaspoon chili powder
- 1/2 teaspoon paprika
- 1/4 teaspoon cayenne pepper (adjust to taste)
- Salt to taste

For the Grilled Corn:

- 4 ears of corn, husked
- Olive oil, for brushing
- Salt and black pepper to taste
- Additional lime wedges for serving (optional)
- Chopped fresh cilantro for garnish (optional)

Instructions:

For the Chili Lime Butter:

1. In a small bowl, combine the softened butter, lime zest, lime juice, chili powder, paprika, cayenne pepper, and salt. Mix until well combined.
2. Taste and adjust the seasoning if needed. Add more chili powder or cayenne pepper for extra heat, or more lime juice for acidity.
3. Transfer the chili lime butter onto a sheet of plastic wrap or parchment paper. Roll it into a log shape and twist the ends to seal.
4. Place the chili lime butter in the refrigerator to chill and firm up while you prepare the corn.

For the Grilled Corn:

1. Preheat your grill to medium-high heat.
2. Brush each ear of corn with olive oil and season with salt and black pepper.

3. Place the corn directly on the grill grates and cook, turning occasionally, until the kernels are charred and tender, about 10-12 minutes.
4. Once the corn is grilled to your liking, remove it from the grill and transfer it to a serving platter.
5. Let the corn cool slightly before serving.
6. Remove the chili lime butter from the refrigerator and slice it into discs.
7. Place a few discs of chili lime butter on each ear of grilled corn, allowing them to melt and coat the kernels.
8. Garnish the corn with chopped fresh cilantro and serve with additional lime wedges on the side if desired.
9. Serve hot and enjoy your delicious grilled corn on the cob with chili lime butter!

This dish is bursting with flavor and makes a wonderful addition to any summer meal.

Feel free to customize the chili lime butter by adding other spices or herbs to suit your taste preferences.

Creamy Mushroom Risotto

Ingredients:

- 1 1/2 cups Arborio rice
- 4 cups chicken or vegetable broth
- 2 tablespoons olive oil
- 1 tablespoon unsalted butter
- 1 small onion, finely chopped
- 2 cloves garlic, minced
- 8 ounces mushrooms (such as cremini or button), sliced
- 1/2 cup dry white wine (optional)
- 1/2 cup grated Parmesan cheese
- Salt and black pepper to taste
- Chopped fresh parsley for garnish (optional)

Instructions:

1. In a saucepan, heat the chicken or vegetable broth over medium heat until it simmers. Reduce the heat to low to keep it warm.
2. In a large skillet or Dutch oven, heat the olive oil and butter over medium heat.
3. Add the chopped onion to the skillet and cook until softened, about 3-4 minutes.
4. Add the minced garlic to the skillet and cook for an additional minute, until fragrant.
5. Add the sliced mushrooms to the skillet and cook, stirring occasionally, until they are golden brown and tender, about 5-7 minutes.
6. Add the Arborio rice to the skillet and stir to coat it with the oil and butter, toasting it slightly, about 2 minutes.
7. If using, pour in the dry white wine and cook, stirring constantly, until it is absorbed by the rice.
8. Begin adding the warm broth to the skillet, one ladleful at a time, stirring frequently. Wait until each ladleful of broth is mostly absorbed before adding the next.
9. Continue adding broth and stirring until the rice is creamy and tender, but still slightly firm to the bite (al dente), about 20-25 minutes. You may not need to use all of the broth.
10. Stir in the grated Parmesan cheese until melted and well combined. Season with salt and black pepper to taste.

11. Remove the skillet from the heat and let the risotto rest for a few minutes before serving.
12. Serve the creamy mushroom risotto hot, garnished with chopped fresh parsley if desired.

Enjoy your delicious and creamy mushroom risotto as a comforting and satisfying meal!

Apple Cinnamon Oatmeal

Ingredients:

- 1 cup old-fashioned rolled oats
- 2 cups water (or milk for a creamier texture)
- 1 apple, peeled, cored, and diced
- 1 tablespoon unsalted butter
- 1 tablespoon brown sugar (or maple syrup)
- 1/2 teaspoon ground cinnamon
- Pinch of salt
- Optional toppings: sliced almonds, chopped walnuts, raisins, sliced bananas, a drizzle of honey or maple syrup

Instructions:

1. In a saucepan, bring the water (or milk) to a boil over medium-high heat.
2. Stir in the rolled oats and reduce the heat to medium-low. Let the oats simmer, stirring occasionally, for about 5 minutes, or until they start to thicken.
3. While the oats are cooking, melt the butter in a skillet over medium heat.
4. Add the diced apple to the skillet and sprinkle with brown sugar, ground cinnamon, and a pinch of salt. Cook, stirring occasionally, for about 5-7 minutes, or until the apples are tender and caramelized.
5. Once the oats are cooked to your desired consistency and the apples are caramelized, remove both from heat.
6. Stir the caramelized apples into the cooked oats until well combined.
7. Taste the oatmeal and adjust the sweetness or cinnamon level if desired.
8. Serve the apple cinnamon oatmeal hot, topped with your favorite toppings such as sliced almonds, chopped walnuts, raisins, sliced bananas, or a drizzle of honey or maple syrup.
9. Enjoy your warm and comforting apple cinnamon oatmeal for a delicious breakfast!

Feel free to customize this recipe by adding other spices like nutmeg or ginger for extra flavor, or by using different types of apples according to your preference. You can also substitute part of the water with apple juice for a stronger apple flavor.

Farmhouse Quiche with Ham and Cheese

Ingredients:

For the Quiche Crust:

- 1 1/4 cups all-purpose flour
- 1/2 teaspoon salt
- 1/2 cup unsalted butter, cold and cut into small cubes
- 3-4 tablespoons ice water

For the Quiche Filling:

- 1 cup diced ham
- 1 cup shredded cheese (such as cheddar, Swiss, or Gruyere)
- 1/4 cup chopped green onions or chives
- 5 large eggs
- 1 cup heavy cream or half-and-half
- Salt and black pepper to taste
- Pinch of nutmeg (optional)

Instructions:

For the Quiche Crust:

1. In a large mixing bowl, combine the all-purpose flour and salt.
2. Add the cold cubed butter to the flour mixture. Using a pastry cutter or your fingers, work the butter into the flour until the mixture resembles coarse crumbs.
3. Gradually add the ice water, one tablespoon at a time, mixing with a fork until the dough comes together and forms a ball. Be careful not to overwork the dough.
4. Shape the dough into a disk, wrap it in plastic wrap, and refrigerate for at least 30 minutes to chill.

For the Quiche Filling:

1. Preheat your oven to 375°F (190°C).
2. On a lightly floured surface, roll out the chilled dough into a circle about 12 inches in diameter. Carefully transfer the rolled-out dough to a 9-inch pie dish. Trim any excess dough hanging over the edges and crimp the edges as desired.

3. Prick the bottom of the crust with a fork to prevent air bubbles from forming during baking. Line the crust with parchment paper and fill it with pie weights or dried beans.
4. Blind bake the crust in the preheated oven for about 10-12 minutes, until it is just starting to set but not yet browned.
5. Remove the parchment paper and pie weights, and continue baking for an additional 5 minutes, until the crust is lightly golden. Remove from the oven and let it cool slightly while you prepare the filling.

Assembling and Baking the Quiche:

1. Spread the diced ham, shredded cheese, and chopped green onions or chives evenly over the bottom of the pre-baked crust.
2. In a separate mixing bowl, whisk together the eggs, heavy cream or half-and-half, salt, black pepper, and nutmeg (if using) until well combined.
3. Pour the egg mixture over the ham, cheese, and onions in the crust, making sure it's evenly distributed.
4. Place the quiche in the preheated oven and bake for 35-40 minutes, or until the filling is set and the top is golden brown.
5. Once done, remove the quiche from the oven and let it cool for a few minutes before slicing and serving.

Enjoy your delicious farmhouse quiche with ham and cheese as a delightful meal any time of the day!

Maple Glazed Bacon

Ingredients:

- 1 pound thick-cut bacon
- 1/4 cup maple syrup
- 1 tablespoon Dijon mustard
- 1 tablespoon apple cider vinegar
- 1/4 teaspoon black pepper
- Optional: pinch of cayenne pepper for a hint of heat

Instructions:

1. Preheat your oven to 375°F (190°C). Line a baking sheet with aluminum foil for easy cleanup.
2. Arrange the bacon slices in a single layer on the prepared baking sheet. Make sure they're not overlapping.
3. In a small bowl, whisk together the maple syrup, Dijon mustard, apple cider vinegar, black pepper, and optional cayenne pepper until well combined.
4. Brush or drizzle the maple glaze over the bacon slices, ensuring each slice is evenly coated.
5. Place the baking sheet in the preheated oven and bake for 15-20 minutes, or until the bacon starts to brown and the edges look crispy.
6. After the initial baking time, carefully remove the baking sheet from the oven and flip the bacon slices over.
7. Brush or drizzle the remaining maple glaze over the other side of the bacon slices.
8. Return the baking sheet to the oven and continue baking for another 10-15 minutes, or until the bacon is crispy and caramelized to your liking.
9. Once done, remove the baking sheet from the oven and transfer the maple glazed bacon to a wire rack to cool slightly and allow the glaze to set.
10. Serve the maple glazed bacon hot as a delicious addition to your breakfast or brunch spread, or enjoy it as a tasty snack any time of the day!

Feel free to customize this recipe by adjusting the amount of maple syrup or adding other seasonings like garlic powder or smoked paprika for extra flavor. Enjoy your sweet and savory maple glazed bacon!

Fresh Garden Salad with Homemade Dressing

Ingredients:

For the Garden Salad:

- Mixed salad greens (such as lettuce, spinach, arugula)
- Cherry tomatoes, halved
- Cucumber, sliced
- Carrots, grated or sliced
- Red onion, thinly sliced
- Bell pepper, diced
- Optional toppings: avocado slices, radishes, croutons, nuts, seeds

For the Homemade Dressing:

- 1/4 cup extra virgin olive oil
- 2 tablespoons balsamic vinegar (or red wine vinegar)
- 1 teaspoon Dijon mustard
- 1 teaspoon honey (or maple syrup)
- 1 clove garlic, minced (optional)
- Salt and black pepper to taste

Instructions:

For the Garden Salad:

1. Wash and prepare all the salad ingredients as needed. Tear or chop the mixed salad greens into bite-sized pieces.
2. In a large salad bowl, combine the mixed salad greens with the cherry tomatoes, cucumber slices, grated carrots, thinly sliced red onion, diced bell pepper, and any other desired toppings.
3. Toss the salad gently to mix all the ingredients together evenly.

For the Homemade Dressing:

1. In a small bowl or jar, combine the extra virgin olive oil, balsamic vinegar, Dijon mustard, honey (or maple syrup), minced garlic (if using), salt, and black pepper.

2. Whisk or shake the dressing vigorously until well combined and emulsified. Taste and adjust the seasoning as needed, adding more salt, pepper, or vinegar to suit your taste preferences.

Assembling the Salad:

1. Drizzle the homemade dressing over the garden salad, starting with a small amount and adding more as needed.
2. Toss the salad gently to coat all the ingredients with the dressing.
3. Taste the salad and adjust the seasoning if needed.
4. Serve the fresh garden salad immediately as a light and healthy meal or side dish.

Feel free to customize the salad and dressing by adding other ingredients like sliced mushrooms, olives, feta cheese, or fresh herbs to suit your taste preferences. Enjoy your delicious and nutritious homemade garden salad with homemade dressing!

Baked Ham with Brown Sugar Glaze

Ingredients:

- 1 bone-in or boneless ham (about 5-7 pounds)
- Whole cloves (optional, for decoration)
- 1/2 cup brown sugar
- 1/4 cup honey
- 2 tablespoons Dijon mustard
- 2 tablespoons apple cider vinegar
- 1/2 teaspoon ground cinnamon
- 1/4 teaspoon ground cloves
- 1/4 teaspoon ground nutmeg

Instructions:

1. Preheat your oven to 325°F (160°C). Line a roasting pan with aluminum foil for easy cleanup.
2. If using a bone-in ham, score the surface of the ham in a diamond pattern with a sharp knife. Insert whole cloves into the center of each diamond, if desired, for decoration.
3. Place the ham in the roasting pan, flat side down.
4. In a small saucepan, combine the brown sugar, honey, Dijon mustard, apple cider vinegar, ground cinnamon, ground cloves, and ground nutmeg. Cook over medium heat, stirring constantly, until the sugar is dissolved and the glaze is smooth, about 3-4 minutes.
5. Brush or pour half of the glaze over the ham, making sure to coat it evenly.
6. Cover the ham loosely with aluminum foil and bake in the preheated oven for about 1 to 1 1/2 hours, depending on the size of the ham. Baste the ham with the pan juices and remaining glaze every 30 minutes.
7. During the last 15-20 minutes of baking, remove the foil to allow the ham to caramelize and develop a golden brown crust.
8. Once the ham reaches an internal temperature of 140°F (60°C) for fully cooked hams or 160°F (71°C) for cook-before-eating hams, remove it from the oven.
9. Let the ham rest for about 10-15 minutes before slicing to allow the juices to redistribute.
10. Serve the baked ham with brown sugar glaze hot, garnished with any remaining pan juices and additional glaze if desired.

11. Enjoy your delicious baked ham with brown sugar glaze as the centerpiece of your meal!

Feel free to customize this recipe by adding other spices or ingredients to the glaze, such as orange zest, ginger, or cloves, to suit your taste preferences.

Butternut Squash Soup with Crispy Sage

Ingredients:

For the Butternut Squash Soup:

- 1 medium butternut squash (about 2 pounds), peeled, seeded, and cubed
- 1 tablespoon olive oil
- 1 onion, chopped
- 2 cloves garlic, minced
- 4 cups vegetable or chicken broth
- 1 teaspoon ground cinnamon
- 1/2 teaspoon ground nutmeg
- Salt and black pepper to taste
- 1/2 cup heavy cream (optional, for creamier soup)

For the Crispy Sage:

- Fresh sage leaves
- 2 tablespoons butter or olive oil
- Salt to taste

Instructions:

For the Butternut Squash Soup:

1. Heat the olive oil in a large pot over medium heat. Add the chopped onion and cook until softened, about 5 minutes.
2. Add the minced garlic to the pot and cook for an additional minute, until fragrant.
3. Add the cubed butternut squash to the pot and cook, stirring occasionally, for about 5 minutes.
4. Pour in the vegetable or chicken broth, ground cinnamon, ground nutmeg, salt, and black pepper. Bring the mixture to a boil, then reduce the heat to low and let it simmer for about 20-25 minutes, or until the squash is tender.
5. Once the squash is cooked, use an immersion blender to puree the soup until smooth. Alternatively, you can carefully transfer the soup in batches to a blender and blend until smooth, then return it to the pot.
6. If using heavy cream, stir it into the soup until well combined. Adjust the seasoning with salt and black pepper to taste.

7. Keep the soup warm over low heat while you prepare the crispy sage.

For the Crispy Sage:

1. In a small skillet, heat the butter or olive oil over medium heat until melted and hot.
2. Add the fresh sage leaves to the skillet in a single layer, making sure not to overcrowd the pan. Cook for about 1-2 minutes per side, until the leaves are crispy and lightly browned.
3. Once crispy, transfer the sage leaves to a plate lined with paper towels to drain. Sprinkle with salt while still warm.

Serving:

1. Ladle the butternut squash soup into bowls.
2. Garnish each bowl of soup with a few crispy sage leaves.
3. Serve hot and enjoy your delicious butternut squash soup with crispy sage!

Feel free to customize this recipe by adding other spices or herbs to the soup, such as ginger, thyme, or rosemary, to suit your taste preferences. You can also skip the heavy cream for a dairy-free version of the soup.

Garlic Butter Shrimp Pasta

Ingredients:

- 8 ounces pasta (such as spaghetti, linguine, or fettuccine)
- 1 pound large shrimp, peeled and deveined
- Salt and black pepper to taste
- 4 tablespoons unsalted butter
- 4 cloves garlic, minced
- 1/4 teaspoon red pepper flakes (optional, for a hint of heat)
- 1/4 cup chicken or vegetable broth
- Juice of 1 lemon
- 1/4 cup chopped fresh parsley
- Grated Parmesan cheese for serving

Instructions:

1. Cook the pasta according to the package instructions in a large pot of salted boiling water until al dente. Drain the pasta, reserving about 1/2 cup of the pasta water, and set aside.
2. Season the shrimp with salt and black pepper to taste.
3. In a large skillet, melt 2 tablespoons of butter over medium heat. Add the minced garlic and red pepper flakes (if using) to the skillet and cook, stirring constantly, for about 1 minute, until fragrant.
4. Add the seasoned shrimp to the skillet and cook for 2-3 minutes on each side, until they are pink and cooked through. Remove the shrimp from the skillet and set aside.
5. In the same skillet, add the remaining 2 tablespoons of butter and chicken or vegetable broth. Bring the mixture to a simmer, scraping up any browned bits from the bottom of the skillet.
6. Return the cooked pasta to the skillet and toss to coat it in the garlic butter sauce. If the sauce is too thick, you can add some of the reserved pasta water to thin it out.
7. Add the cooked shrimp back to the skillet and toss to combine with the pasta.
8. Squeeze the lemon juice over the pasta and shrimp, then sprinkle with chopped fresh parsley.
9. Taste and adjust the seasoning with salt and black pepper if needed.
10. Serve the garlic butter shrimp pasta hot, garnished with grated Parmesan cheese.

Enjoy your delicious garlic butter shrimp pasta as a satisfying and flavorful meal! Feel free to customize this recipe by adding other ingredients like cherry tomatoes, spinach, or mushrooms, according to your taste preferences.

Farmhouse Beef and Vegetable Stew

Ingredients:

- 2 pounds stewing beef, cut into bite-sized pieces
- Salt and black pepper to taste
- 2 tablespoons olive oil
- 1 onion, chopped
- 3 cloves garlic, minced
- 4 cups beef broth
- 1 cup red wine (optional)
- 2 tablespoons tomato paste
- 2 bay leaves
- 1 teaspoon dried thyme
- 1 teaspoon dried rosemary
- 4 carrots, peeled and sliced
- 3 celery stalks, sliced
- 2 large potatoes, peeled and diced
- 1 cup frozen peas
- Chopped fresh parsley for garnish (optional)

Instructions:

1. Season the stewing beef with salt and black pepper to taste.
2. In a large Dutch oven or heavy-bottomed pot, heat the olive oil over medium-high heat. Add the seasoned beef in batches and cook until browned on all sides. Remove the browned beef from the pot and set aside.
3. In the same pot, add the chopped onion and cook until softened, about 5 minutes. Add the minced garlic and cook for an additional minute, until fragrant.
4. Return the browned beef to the pot. Add the beef broth, red wine (if using), tomato paste, bay leaves, dried thyme, and dried rosemary. Stir to combine.
5. Bring the stew to a simmer, then reduce the heat to low. Cover the pot and let the stew cook for 1 1/2 to 2 hours, stirring occasionally, until the beef is tender.
6. Once the beef is tender, add the sliced carrots, sliced celery, and diced potatoes to the pot. Stir to combine.
7. Cover the pot again and let the stew simmer for an additional 30-40 minutes, or until the vegetables are tender and the stew has thickened slightly.
8. Stir in the frozen peas and let them cook for a few minutes until heated through.
9. Taste the stew and adjust the seasoning with salt and black pepper if needed.

10. Remove the bay leaves from the stew before serving.
11. Serve the farmhouse beef and vegetable stew hot, garnished with chopped fresh parsley if desired.

Enjoy your delicious and comforting farmhouse beef and vegetable stew as a satisfying meal! Serve it with crusty bread or over cooked rice or mashed potatoes for a complete meal.

Roasted Brussels Sprouts with Bacon and Balsamic Glaze

Ingredients:

- 1 lb Brussels sprouts, trimmed and halved
- 4 slices bacon, chopped
- 2 tablespoons olive oil
- Salt and black pepper to taste
- 2 tablespoons balsamic vinegar
- 1 tablespoon honey or maple syrup (optional, for sweetness)

Instructions:

1. Preheat your oven to 400°F (200°C). Line a baking sheet with parchment paper or aluminum foil for easy cleanup.
2. In a large mixing bowl, toss the halved Brussels sprouts with olive oil, salt, and black pepper until evenly coated.
3. Spread the Brussels sprouts in a single layer on the prepared baking sheet, cut side down. Arrange the chopped bacon around the Brussels sprouts.
4. Roast the Brussels sprouts and bacon in the preheated oven for about 20-25 minutes, or until the Brussels sprouts are tender and caramelized, and the bacon is crispy.
5. While the Brussels sprouts are roasting, prepare the balsamic glaze. In a small saucepan, combine the balsamic vinegar and honey or maple syrup (if using). Bring the mixture to a simmer over medium heat, then reduce the heat to low and let it simmer for about 10-15 minutes, or until it has thickened and reduced by half. Remove from heat and set aside.
6. Once the Brussels sprouts and bacon are done roasting, transfer them to a serving dish.
7. Drizzle the balsamic glaze over the roasted Brussels sprouts and bacon, tossing gently to coat.
8. Serve the roasted Brussels sprouts with bacon and balsamic glaze hot as a delicious side dish.

Enjoy your flavorful and savory roasted Brussels sprouts with bacon and balsamic glaze! This dish pairs well with roasted chicken, steak, or pork chops, or can be enjoyed on its own as a satisfying vegetable side.

Grilled Chicken Caesar Salad

Ingredients:

For the Grilled Chicken:

- 2 boneless, skinless chicken breasts
- 2 tablespoons olive oil
- 2 cloves garlic, minced
- 1 teaspoon dried oregano
- Salt and black pepper to taste

For the Caesar Salad:

- 1 large head of romaine lettuce, washed and chopped
- 1/2 cup grated Parmesan cheese
- 1 cup croutons (store-bought or homemade)
- Caesar dressing (store-bought or homemade)

For the Caesar Dressing:

- 1/2 cup mayonnaise
- 2 tablespoons grated Parmesan cheese
- 2 tablespoons freshly squeezed lemon juice
- 1 tablespoon Dijon mustard
- 2 cloves garlic, minced
- 2 anchovy fillets, minced (optional)
- Salt and black pepper to taste
- 2 tablespoons olive oil

Instructions:

For the Grilled Chicken:

1. In a small bowl, whisk together the olive oil, minced garlic, dried oregano, salt, and black pepper to make the marinade.
2. Place the chicken breasts in a resealable plastic bag or shallow dish, and pour the marinade over them. Seal the bag or cover the dish, and let the chicken marinate in the refrigerator for at least 30 minutes, or up to 4 hours.

3. Preheat your grill to medium-high heat. Remove the chicken from the marinade, discarding any excess marinade.
4. Grill the chicken breasts for 6-8 minutes per side, or until cooked through and no longer pink in the center. The internal temperature should reach 165°F (75°C). Remove the chicken from the grill and let it rest for a few minutes before slicing.

For the Caesar Dressing:

1. In a small bowl, whisk together the mayonnaise, grated Parmesan cheese, lemon juice, Dijon mustard, minced garlic, anchovy fillets (if using), salt, and black pepper.
2. Slowly drizzle in the olive oil while whisking continuously, until the dressing is smooth and well combined. Taste and adjust the seasoning if needed. If the dressing is too thick, you can thin it out with a little water.

Assembling the Salad:

1. In a large mixing bowl, toss the chopped romaine lettuce with the Caesar dressing until evenly coated.
2. Divide the dressed lettuce among serving plates or bowls.
3. Top each serving of lettuce with slices of grilled chicken.
4. Sprinkle grated Parmesan cheese over the chicken.
5. Garnish the salads with croutons.
6. Serve the grilled chicken Caesar salad immediately, and enjoy!

Feel free to customize your salad by adding additional toppings such as cherry tomatoes, sliced cucumbers, or avocado slices.

Farm-Fresh Blueberry Muffins

Ingredients:

- 1 1/2 cups all-purpose flour
- 3/4 cup granulated sugar
- 1/2 teaspoon salt
- 2 teaspoons baking powder
- 1/3 cup vegetable oil or melted butter
- 1 large egg
- 1/3 cup milk
- 1 teaspoon vanilla extract
- 1 cup fresh blueberries
- Optional: Turbinado sugar for sprinkling on top

Instructions:

1. Preheat your oven to 375°F (190°C). Line a muffin tin with paper liners or grease the muffin cups with butter or cooking spray.
2. In a large mixing bowl, whisk together the flour, sugar, salt, and baking powder until well combined.
3. In a separate bowl, whisk together the vegetable oil or melted butter, egg, milk, and vanilla extract until smooth.
4. Pour the wet ingredients into the dry ingredients and stir until just combined. Be careful not to overmix, as this can lead to dense muffins.
5. Gently fold in the fresh blueberries until evenly distributed throughout the batter.
6. Divide the batter evenly among the prepared muffin cups, filling each about two-thirds full.
7. If desired, sprinkle the tops of the muffins with a little turbinado sugar for added sweetness and crunch.
8. Bake the muffins in the preheated oven for 18-20 minutes, or until they are golden brown and a toothpick inserted into the center comes out clean.
9. Remove the muffins from the oven and let them cool in the muffin tin for a few minutes before transferring them to a wire rack to cool completely.
10. Serve the farm-fresh blueberry muffins warm or at room temperature, and enjoy!

These muffins are best enjoyed the day they are made, but you can store any leftovers in an airtight container at room temperature for up to 2 days, or in the refrigerator for up to 5 days. Warm them briefly in the microwave before serving if desired.

Sweet and Spicy Barbecue Ribs

Ingredients:

For the Ribs:

- 2 racks of baby back ribs (about 4-5 pounds total)
- Salt and black pepper to taste
- 2 tablespoons brown sugar

For the Sweet and Spicy Barbecue Sauce:

- 1 cup ketchup
- 1/2 cup apple cider vinegar
- 1/4 cup honey
- 2 tablespoons Worcestershire sauce
- 2 tablespoons Dijon mustard
- 2 cloves garlic, minced
- 1 teaspoon smoked paprika
- 1/2 teaspoon cayenne pepper (adjust to taste)
- Salt and black pepper to taste

Instructions:

For the Ribs:

1. Preheat your oven to 275°F (135°C). Line a large baking sheet with aluminum foil for easy cleanup.
2. Remove the membrane from the back of the ribs by sliding a knife under the membrane and then pulling it off. This step ensures that the ribs will be tender and flavorful.
3. Season the ribs generously with salt, black pepper, and brown sugar, rubbing the seasonings into the meat.
4. Place the seasoned ribs on the prepared baking sheet, meat side up.
5. Cover the ribs tightly with another sheet of aluminum foil, sealing the edges to create a packet.
6. Bake the ribs in the preheated oven for 2 1/2 to 3 hours, or until the meat is tender and starting to pull away from the bones.

For the Sweet and Spicy Barbecue Sauce:

1. In a medium saucepan, combine all the barbecue sauce ingredients: ketchup, apple cider vinegar, honey, Worcestershire sauce, Dijon mustard, minced garlic, smoked paprika, cayenne pepper, salt, and black pepper.
2. Stir well to combine all the ingredients.
3. Bring the sauce to a simmer over medium heat, then reduce the heat to low and let it simmer for about 10-15 minutes, stirring occasionally, until the sauce has thickened slightly and the flavors have melded together.
4. Taste the sauce and adjust the seasoning if needed. Add more honey for sweetness or more cayenne pepper for extra heat.

For Assembling and Grilling:

1. Preheat your grill to medium-high heat.
2. Remove the foil from the baked ribs and brush them generously with the sweet and spicy barbecue sauce, coating both sides.
3. Place the sauced ribs on the preheated grill and cook for about 5-7 minutes per side, or until they are caramelized and slightly charred, brushing with more barbecue sauce as needed.
4. Once done, remove the ribs from the grill and let them rest for a few minutes before serving.

Serve the sweet and spicy barbecue ribs hot, sliced between the bones, and enjoy the delicious combination of sweet, tangy, and spicy flavors! These ribs pair well with coleslaw, cornbread, or grilled vegetables for a complete meal.

Pumpkin Pie with Whipped Cream

Ingredients:

For the Pumpkin Pie Filling:

- 1 (15-ounce) can pumpkin puree (not pumpkin pie filling)
- 3/4 cup granulated sugar
- 1 teaspoon ground cinnamon
- 1/2 teaspoon ground ginger
- 1/4 teaspoon ground cloves
- 1/2 teaspoon ground nutmeg
- 1/2 teaspoon salt
- 2 large eggs
- 1 cup evaporated milk or heavy cream
- 1 unbaked pie crust (store-bought or homemade)

For the Whipped Cream:

- 1 cup heavy cream, chilled
- 2 tablespoons powdered sugar
- 1 teaspoon vanilla extract

Instructions:

For the Pumpkin Pie:

1. Preheat your oven to 425°F (220°C). Place a baking sheet in the oven to preheat as well. This will help ensure that the bottom of the pie crust cooks evenly.
2. In a large mixing bowl, combine the pumpkin puree, granulated sugar, ground cinnamon, ground ginger, ground cloves, ground nutmeg, and salt. Mix until well combined.
3. Add the eggs to the pumpkin mixture and beat until smooth.
4. Gradually add the evaporated milk or heavy cream to the pumpkin mixture, stirring until fully incorporated.
5. Pour the pumpkin pie filling into the unbaked pie crust, spreading it out evenly.
6. Place the pie on the preheated baking sheet in the oven.

7. Bake the pie at 425°F (220°C) for 15 minutes, then reduce the oven temperature to 350°F (175°C) and continue baking for an additional 40-50 minutes, or until the filling is set and a knife inserted near the center comes out clean.
8. Once done, remove the pie from the oven and let it cool completely on a wire rack before slicing and serving.

For the Whipped Cream:

1. In a chilled mixing bowl, combine the chilled heavy cream, powdered sugar, and vanilla extract.
2. Using an electric mixer or whisk, beat the cream mixture on medium-high speed until soft peaks form. Be careful not to overmix, or you'll end up with butter!
3. Once the pie has cooled, slice it into wedges and serve each slice with a dollop of freshly whipped cream.

Enjoy your delicious pumpkin pie with whipped cream as a delightful dessert for any occasion, especially during the fall and holiday season!

www.ingramcontent.com/pod-product-compliance
Lightning Source LLC
LaVergne TN
LVHW061944070526
838199LV00060B/3975